Town Life

Tony D. Triggs

Wayland

Titles in the series

Country Life

Exploration

Kings and Queens

Religion

Scientists and Writers

Town Life

Cover illustrations: *Background* Seventeenth-century map of Chester; *Inset* The Tower of London and shipping, 15th century.

First published in 1993 by Wayland (Publishers) Ltd
61 Western Road, Hove, East Sussex BN3 1JD, England

Editor: Cath Senker
Designer: John Christopher
Picture Researcher: Tony D. Triggs
Consultant: Linda Goddard, Primary History Advisory Teacher, Runnymede Staff Development Centre, Surrey

British Library Cataloguing in Publication Data
Triggs, Tony D.
  Town Life. – (Tudors and Stuarts series)
  I. Title II. Series
  942

ISBN 0-7502-0689-6

Typeset by Strong Silent Type
Printed and bound by B.P.C.C. Paulton Books, Great Britain

Notes for teachers

Town Life draws on a wide range of exciting sources, including maps, artefacts, drawings and inventories. This book:

◆ looks at the different kinds of towns in Tudor and Stuart times and examines one Tudor town in detail using a contemporary map;

◆ helps the reader to identify buildings and streets in his or her town that date from Tudor and Stuart times;

◆ discusses the different kinds of work people did in towns;

◆ examines the effects of the plague of 1665 and the Fire of London;

◆ helps the reader to understand how to use clues from the past, such as quotations, inventories and maps, to learn about how people lived in Tudor and Stuart times.

Picture acknowledgements
L & R Adkins 10 (below), 19 (above), 21 (above), 26 (above); Bodleian Library (ref G.A. f B74) 13 (below); British Library (ref Cott Aug I i 74) 6-7, (ref Crace Port II 53) 25; Bridgeman Art Library *cover* (inset) and title page; David Williams Picture Library 9 (above); C M Dixon 4, 27 (below); E T Archive 24; Mary Evans 19 (below); Mansell 17, 27 (above); The Masters and Fellows of Magdalene College, Cambridge 14, 26 (below); National Maritime Museum 20-21 (below); National Museum of Wales 11; National Trust 10 (above); NHPA (S Dalton) 22 (above); Ann Ronan 13 (above); Shakespeare Birthplace Trust 16; Skyscan 9 (below) 20 (above); Syndication International (courtesy of His Grace the Archbishop of Canterbury & the Trustees of Lambeth Palace) 18; Topham *cover* (background), 8; Wayland 22 (below), 23; York Archaeological Trust 15. Artwork: John Yates 5, 12.

Contents

The main towns

The Tudor kings and queens ruled England and Wales
from 1485 to 1603, and the Stuarts ruled England,
Scotland and Wales from 1603 to 1714.

In Tudor times many villages grew into
small towns. Sometimes this happened
because people met in a certain village
to buy and sell food. The village grew in
importance and many people went to
live there.

There was often an open space in the
middle of a town for a market, and some
of these open spaces are still used for
markets today.

The size of towns

Nowadays there is a census every ten
years. In a census, the government
counts the people in each town and
village. Britain had its first census in 1801.

**The market cross in Chichester. There used to
be a market-place here in Tudor times.**

The Tudors and Stuarts did not have censuses, so we have to use other evidence to find out the size of different places. In early Tudor times, an Italian wrote that England had hardly any big towns apart from London. However, he mentioned 'Bristol in the west and ... York, which is on the border with Scotland'. York is really a long way from Scotland, and this reminds us to use evidence carefully.

The biggest towns

In Tudor times the government worked out how much tax each town should pay. It also counted the number of men in each town who were fit enough to fight if war broke out. Clues like this show that London was the biggest town of all. It had about 50,000 people. The next biggest towns were Edinburgh, Norwich, Newcastle-upon-Tyne, Bristol and Coventry. Newcastle had about 1,700 fit young men, so perhaps you can estimate how many people it had altogether.

Some of our modern cities, such as Birmingham, had not begun to grow at all. They were still villages.

This map shows the biggest towns in Britain in Tudor times.

A town in detail

The painting on these pages was done by a Tudor artist. It shows what the town of Great Yarmouth was like in Tudor times. It was built near the mouth of a river, and it became a very important port in Tudor and Stuart times.

KEY

1 This magnificent building reminds us that the Church was rich and powerful in Tudor times. What sort of buildings might be even bigger today?

2 Fishermen's nets being hung up to dry.

3 A well where people got their water. Perhaps you can see some women carrying water home.

4 The town had walls and guns to keep attackers out. Find the guns and try to decide why the town council put them in that position.

5 A crane for unloading coal and other goods from ships.

6 Ships and windmills had sails to catch the wind.

7 The market-place. There is still a busy market there today.

8 Most travellers went on horseback or on foot.

9 What do you think this object is? (No one is sure.)

Trade and fine buildings

Busy towns had fine buildings, which were used for many different purposes. There were indoor markets, buildings where unsold goods were stored, and halls where traders and other workers met. There were also buildings where tax officials collected money. Some of these buildings can still be seen in our towns today.

Guilds

Traders in Tudor times often belonged to guilds. Guilds were like modern trade unions. Each group of traders had a guild of its own, and the traders expected the guild to look after them.

Many towns had dyers and bleachers who coloured cloth before it was cut up and made into clothes. They expected their guild to stop outsiders from coming to the town and taking away their trade by doing similar work.

Butchers, bakers and other workers expected their guilds to protect them in the same way.

In many towns we can still see the hall where members of the guilds used to hold their meetings.

A photograph of the guildhall at Thaxted in Essex.

Street names remind us of the jobs people did and the things they sold. Baker Street in London was named after the bakers who lived and worked there.

The Shambles in York got its name from the shambles (tables) where butchers cut up their meat. Why do you think the members of each guild gathered together in one street?

(Below) A photograph showing the tollhouse at St Fagans, Wales.

(Above) The butter cross at Culross, Scotland, today. People used to gather around it to buy and sell butter, eggs and cheese.

Traders taking goods in and out of a town had to go to the tollhouse to pay a toll, or tax. The building at the front of the picture on the left, with the three-cornered roof, is a tollhouse.

Houses

Some towns grew up as centres for trade in wool or cloth. These included Oswestry and Shrewsbury in Shropshire, and Lavenham, Boston and Hadleigh in East Anglia. Wool merchants often became very rich, and we can still see their magnificent houses in some of these places.

(Right) A Tudor merchant's house in Coggeshall, Essex.

This fine sixteenth-century house stands in Stirling in Scotland.

Different ways of building

The Tudors built most of their houses out of wood. They put up a framework of wooden beams, then they filled the gaps between them with sticks and covered the sticks with mud or plaster.

One of the houses on this page was built of stone. Can you pick it out? The Stuarts used stone far more than the Tudors. Perhaps you can find out some reasons for this.

Inside people's houses

When people died, their friends or family sometimes made a list of all the things they had owned. We still have some of these lists today. If we know what people owned we can start to imagine the sort of lives they led.

In 1525 a Londoner called John Port died, and his friends found the following things in his house:

The bedroom in a seventeenth-century Tudor house in Wales.

In the hall [main room]:

A hanging [tapestry], 10 yards long [nearly 10 metres]
The curtain of the window
A table top with a pair of tressels [supports]
4 stools and 2 close chairs [chairs with chamberpots]
A pair of tongs, a poker and a little shovel

In the parlour:

A hanging, 37 yards
6 paintings and a little one
6 cushions made in Belgium
A round table
An old sideboard

A pair of andirons [metal objects to support a log for the fireplace]
4 old books and an inkstand
2 axes and a bell
4 old axes
2 shields
A pair of old card tables

In the pantry:

6 large candlesticks
A pair of tongs, a fire shovel, a poker and a chopping knife
[All sorts of pots and pans]

In his bedroom:

A hanging, 50 yards
A four-poster bed with 3 curtains

A pair of woollen sheets
An old cupboard with a desk
A square oak chest with a holy cross and a valuable cloth
A candlestick
A number of chests
An old close chair and a stool
A pair of andirons

There were two more bedrooms and another room full of clothes belonging to Port and his wife. (Some of her things had been damaged by moths.) The house had two storeys and there was also an attic full of 'lumber' [junk] under the sloping roof. There was a downstairs room called a shop, but it only contained odds and ends when Port died.

Working life in a country town

Townspeople used many things that came from local farms. Leicester and Northampton were near to rich pastures – fields where cattle ate the grass. Cattle grew fat on the pastures, then they were driven to Leicester to be killed and cut up by the many butchers who lived in the town. The cattle skins were made into leather.

Pie charts showing the work people did in Northampton, Leicester and Coventry.

Some of the leather was sent to Northampton, where craftsmen used it to make saddles, shoes and other goods. Leather shoes are still made in the town.

The pie charts below show the work people did in three English towns in about 1580. How do the ones for Northampton and Leicester match what you have read about them? What was the main work in Coventry?

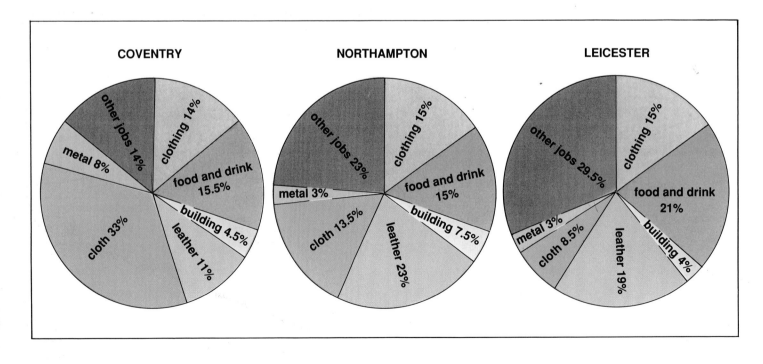

COVENTRY

other jobs 14%
clothing 14%
metal 8%
food and drink 15.5%
building 4.5%
cloth 33%
leather 11%

NORTHAMPTON

other jobs 23%
clothing 15%
metal 3%
food and drink 15%
building 7.5%
cloth 13.5%
leather 23%

LEICESTER

other jobs 29.5%
clothing 15%
food and drink 21%
metal 3%
building 4%
cloth 8.5%
leather 19%

(Above) **Working life was hard for many people. This woman is using bellows to make a fire burn more fiercely.**

Town and country

If you look at the map of Windsor you will see how small it was, with fields all around it. Leicester was very similar. Many townspeople grew their own wheat in the nearby fields. The local miller ground it into flour, and the people used the flour to make loaves of bread. They baked the bread in public ovens which everyone shared.

The fields were so near the town that the smell of hay and cattle dung must have mixed with the smell of the baking bread.

(Below) **A seventeenth-century map of Windsor.**

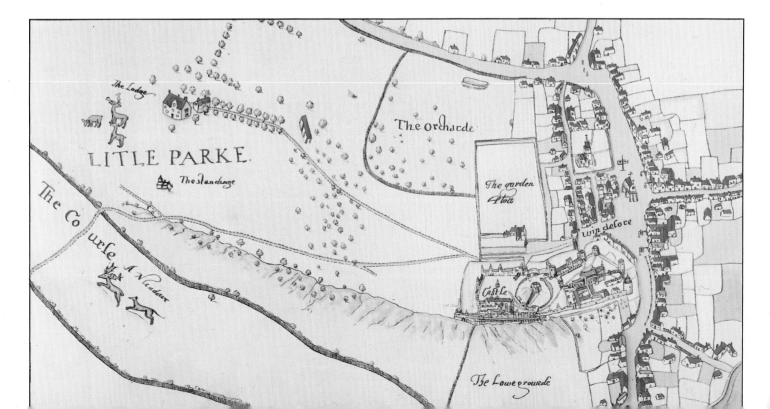

Life in large towns

Some towns became large and famous because of a local industry. Newcastle-upon-Tyne grew because there were coal and lead mines very near the town. Ships called there and took the coal and lead to customers throughout the country.

Clues in a picture

Look at the woman in the picture on the left.
Do you think she was rich or poor? Perhaps you can also decide whether it was summer or winter. Why do you think she was wearing a mask?

This woman lived in Newcastle-upon-Tyne in the 1640s.

A very old street

There is a street in York called The Shambles. Most of the buildings there were built in Tudor and Stuart times. If you can't remember who used to work there, look again at page 9. Do you think the street was smart and clean or do you think it was smelly and dirty?

Words can remind us about the past. What do we mean when we say that something is a shambles?

Clues we can read

London was the largest, busiest town, and some people disliked the noise and fuss. According to one man:

" In every street carts and coaches make such a thundering. Hammers are beating, pots clinking. There are porters sweating under burdens, and merchants carrying bags of money. "

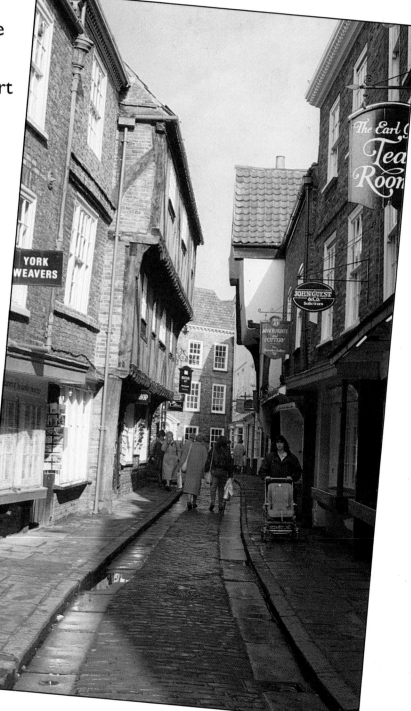

The Shambles in York today.

Children

In Tudor and Stuart times very few children went to school. Most schools charged fees, and very few families could afford them. Some families in towns ran successful businesses and became wealthy. Rich parents often sent their sons to school, but they kept their daughters at home to do housework.

The classroom in Stratford-upon-Avon grammar school where Shakespeare used to study.

Going to school

William Shakespeare lived from 1564 to 1616. He grew up in a busy town called Stratford-upon-Avon. His father was the mayor, and he also ran a glove-making business. He sent William to the local school, where the boys spent most of their time learning Latin poems by heart. There was only one teacher, who beat the boys when they got the words wrong.

On the left you can see the inside of Stratford-upon-Avon grammar school, where Shakespeare studied when he was young. Try to imagine what lessons were like in a room like this, and compare it with your own classroom.

Apprentices

Boys in towns often became apprentices. This means that they became unpaid helpers in a workshop. By the time they had grown up they knew enough about the job to open a workshop of their own. Boys became apprentices when they were about ten years old (or fourteen if they had been to school).

Timeline

1550–1600
Many villages start to hold markets; they grow rapidly.

1594–1613
Shakespeare writes his plays in London.

Shakespeare's father probably needed his help in the family glove-making business but Shakespeare became a playwright (someone who writes plays). In his play *As You Like It* Shakespeare wrote about:

The apprentice at the front is learning how to make gloves.

> " *… the whining school boy,*
> *with his satchel*
> *And shining morning face,*
> *creeping like snail*
> *Unwillingly to school.* "

Perhaps Shakespeare was thinking of his own schooldays!

The poor

People who lived in villages often rented their houses and their land. Rents rose during the time of the Tudor kings and queens. Many villagers could not afford to pay the rent so they left and looked for work in the towns. Jobs were very hard to find, and some of them had to beg for money on the streets.

A Tudor drawing of women being hanged.

Clues in a rhyme

Historians find clues in all sorts of writing. A nursery rhyme that was written in the sixteenth century says:

> " *Hark, hark,*
> *The dogs do bark,*
> *The beggars are coming to town;*
> *Some in rags,*
> *And some in jags [tatty clothes],*
> *And one in a velvet gown.* "

Many historians think this refers to the homeless people from the countryside. It sounds as if someone has given a beggar a smart gown to wear, but townspeople usually treated beggars very harshly.

If poor people stole or did anything else that was wrong they were punished severely. We know about these harsh punishments from pictures that were drawn at the time.

The men in the picture below have been put in stocks, a heavy wooden frame with holes in it. They have had their hands and feet (or just their hands) locked in the holes.

Whitgift's almshouses (homes for the poor) can still be seen in Croydon, Surrey.

Men being punished by being locked in stocks.

Helping the poor

A few wealthy people tried to help the poor by giving them homes. A bishop called William Whitgift paid for the houses in the picture above, which were built in 1596–9. Through the gateway there is a patch of grass with thirty-two small homes all around it. They were for sixteen women and sixteen men who were very poor.

Towns with castles

Some towns grew up near castles or fortresses. Plymouth and Deal, in the south of England, are both very good examples of this. On the right you can see Walmer Castle, near Deal. Henry VIII had the castle built in 1539. Plymouth also had docks where warships were built and repaired.

Walmer Castle. You can see that it was built to be strong.

War and work

In 1588 the Spanish Armada (fleet of warships) sailed into the English Channel. The Spaniards were planning to conquer England but an English fleet sailed out of Plymouth and chased and attacked them. Gale force winds helped the English to drive the Spaniards away. Later, the English made medals and special playing cards to show what had happened.

These English playing cards show how the Spanish Armada was beaten.

The Admirall ye Ld Sheffeild St Tho: Howard and others joyn with Drake and Fenez agt ye Spanish Fleet & worst them.

The Spaniards on sight of the Fireships weighing Ancors cutting Cables and betakeing themselves to flight wth a hideouse noise & in great Confusion.

8 Fireships Sent by ye English Admirall towards ye Spanish fleet in ye Middle of ye night under the Conduct of young and Prowse.

A modern picture of boys preparing an Elizabethan cannon for firing.

All young men were expected to fight if there was a war, and in Tudor times many towns had butts (targets) where they could practise with bows and arrows. The soldiers at castles had other weapons, including cannons. Sailors also had many cannons on their warships. Towns like Plymouth were busy because the ships and weapons needed a lot of repairs and supplies.

One way to learn about the past is to try things out. The photograph above was taken at Portland Castle in Dorset. The boys are finding out what it is like to get cannon ready for firing.

The plague

London was a very unhealthy place. Farmers drove cattle into the city and butchers killed them on the spot. The blood and bits of unwanted meat went bad and stank. Rats lived in the filth, and the fleas on the rats spread germs to human beings. This caused a dreadful disease called the plague. In 1665 it killed nearly half the people in London.

(Above) A rat in a drainage pipe. Rats are still a threat to health today.

(Below) People fleeing from the plague in 1630. The skeletons stand for death. Why do you think one of them is holding an hourglass (a thing like an egg timer)?

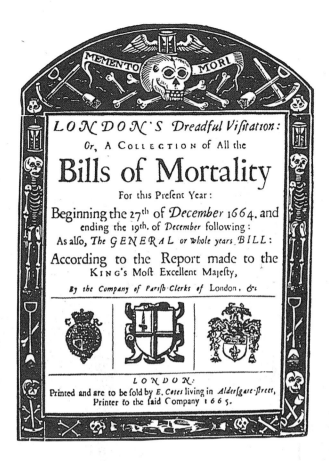

The front page of a collection of Bills of Mortality. During the plague a new bill was issued every week, listing all the new deaths and giving the reasons.

Escaping from the plague

If someone in a house had the plague, the family put a cross on the door to warn other people to stay away. A cart went round the streets to collect the dead bodies. The bodies were dumped in huge pits because no one had time to dig graves for them all.

Those who had homes in the countryside fled from the city in panic. Death was like an enemy who was chasing them and trying to catch them.

Artists sometimes showed death as a skeleton. The skeleton seemed to be everywhere at once, killing anyone it could catch. Some of the people who fled from the city still died of the plague, which spread to many towns and villages.

New laws, cleaner towns

Historians like to see how big events change people's lives. Before the plague, people put up with dirt and rats in their towns. Afterwards, they tried much harder to keep their towns clean.

In Skipton, Yorkshire, a new law was passed. It said that people would be punished severely if they dared to put any 'dung, carrion [bad meat] or other stinking dirt in the road'.

The Fire of London

In 1666 a dreadful fire destroyed half of London. It burned for five days and nights. According to a writer called Samuel Pepys:

> *" the flames were like a blood-coloured wall a mile [1½ km] wide. The wall of fire moved across the city, destroying everything in its way. "*

Out of control

The fire began in a baker's shop in Pudding Lane. The houses and shops burned easily because they were built mainly of wood. To make matters worse, the fire leapt quickly from street to street because the houses were very close together.

A painting of the Fire of London, done around the time of the fire.

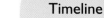

Pepys told the Mayor of London to start pulling rows of houses down to stop the fire spreading. 'We've been doing that,' the Mayor replied, 'but the fire overtakes us faster than we can pull them down.'

This map of London, Westminster and Southwark in 1690 shows how the city was rebuilt after the fire.

Rebuilding the city

After the fire, much of London had to be rebuilt. The new streets were wider, and most of the buildings were made of stone. This helped to prevent any more dreadful fires. The city was also cleaner and less overcrowded than before the plague. Although the disease broke out again, it was never as bad as it had been in 1665.

1535–45
Henry VIII has several castles and battleships built.

1588
The English navy defeats the Spanish Armada.

1665
The plague strikes London.

1666
The Fire of London.

Entertainment

There were plenty of ways for people in towns to enjoy themselves. There were places where they could eat and drink, and theatres where they could go to watch the latest plays. There were also travelling entertainers who visited towns and performed in the street.

(Right) Modern dancers trying out a Tudor dance. They are wearing the kind of clothes Tudor dancers used to wear.

**(Left)
A printed song from Stuart times.**

Coffee houses

In Stuart times most towns had cafés called coffee houses. Coffee and tobacco had been discovered in foreign countries in the sixteenth century. They were very expensive to buy in Britain, but men in towns were keen to try them if they could afford it. Women did not usually go to coffee houses, so we do not often see them in pictures like the one on the right.

(Above) The inside of a Stuart coffee house. Perhaps you can see what the men are using to smoke their tobacco.

(Above) This painting, from about 1620, shows a woman relaxing and smoking a pipe.

Women were expected to stay at home looking after their children and helping with the family business. They probably had less chance to rest and enjoy themselves than men did.

Timeline

1480	1500	1520	1540	1560	1580

Tudors

1485 HENRY VII

1509 HENRY VIII

1547 EDWARD VI

1553 MARY TUDOR

1558 ELIZABETH I

1480–1500	1500–1520	1520–1540	1540–1560	1560–1580	1580–1600
1492 Columbus sails to America.	**1500–1547** Sheep farmers enclose common land.	**1520** The Spaniards begin to settle on the American mainland.	**1543** The Belgian-born scientist Andreas Vesalius publishes his book about the human body.	**1567** As a Catholic, Mary Queen of Scots flees from Scotland but is imprisoned in England.	**1587** Mary Queen of Scots is executed.
	1509 Cabot tries to sail round the north of Canada.	**1534** Henry VIII becomes Head of the Church in England and Wales.	**1547–1553** Many schools and colleges are built.	**1577** Sir Francis Drake sets off on his voyage around the world.	**1588** The Spanish Armada is defeated.
	1500 – 1600 Rents rise and many poor villagers move to the towns to look for work.	**1536** Henry VIII's second wife, Anne Boleyn, is put to death.	**1549** Robert Kett leads a rebellion in Norfolk.		**1595** Sir Walter Raleigh explores South America.
		1539 Henry VIII has the monasteries destroyed.	**1550 – 1650** Newcastle grows because of the coal and lead mines.		**1590–1616** William Shakespeare writes his plays.
			1553–1558 Protestants are persecuted and put to death.		

1600   1620   1640   1660   1680   1700

Stuarts

1603 JAMES I (JAMES VI OF SCOTLAND)

1625 CHARLES I

1649–1660 COMMONWEALTH
1653 OLIVER CROMWELL
1658 RICHARD CROMWELL
1660 CHARLES II

1685 JAMES II
1688 WILLIAM III & MARY II

1702–1714 ANNE

1600–1620	1620–1640	1640–1660	1660–1680	1680–1700	1700–1710
1605 The Gunpowder Plot.	**1628** The scientist William Harvey describes how blood goes round the body.	**1642** The Civil War begins.	**1665** The plague.	**1690** The Battle of the Boyne.	**1707** England and Scotland are officially united.
1607 The explorer Henry Hudson sets off to the coast of northern Canada.	**1630–1641** Charles I rules without Parliament.	**1646** Charles I is captured and imprisoned.	**1666** The Great Fire of London.	**1694** Queen Mary dies.	
1610 Hudson discovers a huge bay in northern Canada. It is named after him.		**1649** Charles I is executed.	**1660–1669** Samuel Pepys writes his diary about life during the Restoration.	**1667–1695** The composer Henry Purcell writes his music.	
1620 The Puritan Pilgrim Fathers sail from England to settle in America.		**1649–1660** England, Scotland and Wales are ruled without a king or queen.	**1660–1685** Scientists Robert Hooke and Isaac Newton study light and gravity. Sir Christopher Wren designs many buildings in London.		
		1660 The Restoration of the monarchy. Charles II becomes king.	**1660–1700** Coffee houses become popular.		

Glossary

Beams Long, strong pieces of wood that were often used by Tudor builders.

Bleacher Someone whose job is to make cloth pale or white.

Census A careful count of all the people in a certain country.

Council A group of people who make rules for the town where they live.

Dock A place where ships tie up when they are in port. Ships are also built or mended in the dock.

Dyer A person whose job is to colour cloth.

Fortress A building or area surrounded by strong, high walls to stop attackers entering.

Framework A wooden frame forming part of a building.

Guildhall The place where a guild used to meet.

Industry The main work in a town.

Lead A soft metal that used to be used for covering roofs and making pipes.

Leather The skin from cattle, treated so that it can be used to make things like shoes and bags.

Merchant A trader.

Plague A serious disease that humans can catch from rats, and which spreads very easily.

Plaster A thick mixture of lime, sand and water, used to cover walls and ceilings.

Porter Someone whose job is to carry things.

Saddle A seat for the rider of a horse.

Tax Money that people have to give to the government.

Tollhouse The place where traders had to pay a toll for bringing goods in or out of a town.

Trade The buying or selling of goods.

Books to read

Blackwood, A. *Recreation in History* (Wayland, 1984)

Carter, M., Culpin, C. & Kinloch, N. *Past into Present 2: 1400 – 1700* (Collins Educational, 1990)

Jessop, J. *Tudor Towns* (Wayland, 1990)

Kelly, R. & T. *Oxford: A City at War* (Thornes & Hulton, 1987)

Kelly, T. *Children in Tudor England* (Thornes & Hulton, 1987)

Regan, G. *Elizabethan England* (Batsford, 1990)

Steel, B. & Steel, A. *Tudor Merchant* (Wayland, 1986)

Triggs, T.D. *Tudor and Stuart Times* (Folens, 1992)

Wood, T. *The Stuarts* (Paperbird, 1991)

Places to visit

Cambridge
The colleges and other buildings.
Canterbury, Kent
Almshouses – houses that were built for the poor.
Cardiff
National Museum of Wales, Welsh Folk Museum, St Fagans, near Cardiff
Croydon, Surrey
The almshouses built by William Whitgift.
London
The Museum of London, Barbican

Shrewsbury, Shropshire
There are various buildings from Tudor and Stuart times such as Rowley's House (a Tudor merchant's house) and the public library, which is in the building of a Tudor grammar school.
Stratford-upon-Avon, Warwickshire
There are various buildings, including the grammar school where Shakespeare studied.
York
The streets called The Shambles and Pavement, and buildings such as the ruins of a monastery destroyed at the time of Henry VIII.

Index

Words in **bold** indicate subjects that are shown in pictures as well as in the text.